Art Works™ Drawing Robots

Carolyn Scrace

SCRIBBLERS

Author:
Carolyn Scrace graduated from Brighton College of Art, UK, with a focus on design and illustration. She has since worked in animation, advertising and children's publishing. She has a special interest in natural history and has written many books on the subject, including *Lion Journal* and *Gorilla Journal* in the *Animal Journal* series.

How to use this book:

Follow the easy, numbered instructions. Simple step-by-step stages enable budding young artists to create their own amazing drawings.

What you will need:

1. Paper.
2. Wax crayons.
3. Felt-tip pens to add colour.

Published in Great Britain in MMXV by
Scribblers, a division of Book House
25 Marlborough Place, Brighton BN1 1UB
www.salariya.com
www.book-house.co.uk

ISBN-13: 978-1-910184-85-1

1 3 5 7 9 8 6 4 2

A CIP catalogue record for this book is available from the British Library.

Printed and bound in China.

Contents

Clunk!

control panel

1 Clunk needs a head,

2 ...a body and a control panel,

3 ...two legs and feet,

4 ...one small arm and hand,

5 ...and one **big** arm and hand!

6 Draw in his eyes, nose and mouth.

4

Draw in his two antennae.

Add crayoned stripes to Clunk's arms.

Finish drawing his eyes and mouth.

Add some dials and stripes to his control panel.

Colour in with felt-tip pens.

5

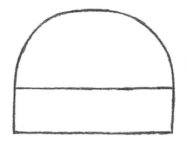

Click!

1 Click needs a **big** head,

2 ...a body,

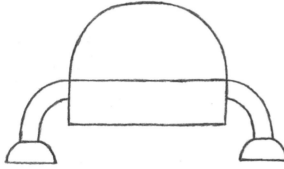

3 ...two arms and hands,

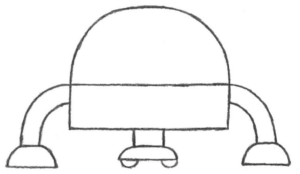

4 ...and a leg with two wheels.

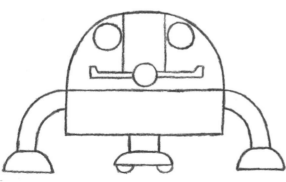

5 Add two eyes and a mouth,

Aerial

6 ...and draw in her squiggly aerial.

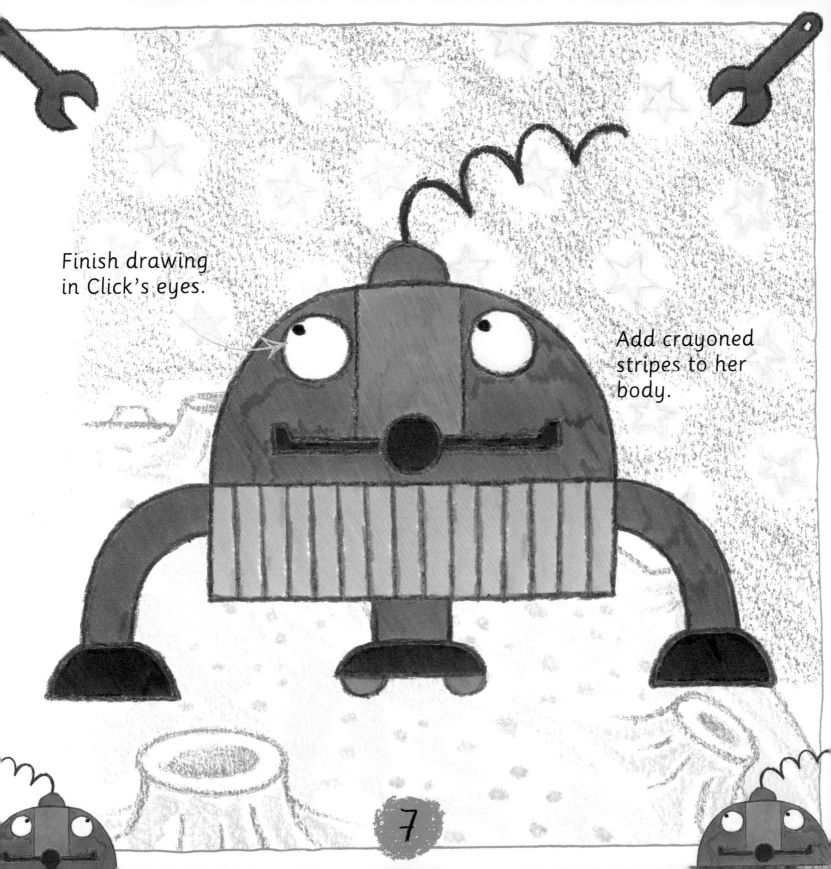

Finish drawing
in Click's eyes.

Add crayoned
stripes to her
body.

7

Buzz!

control panels

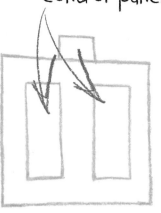

1 Buzz needs a very, very small head,

2 ...a **big** body with two control panels,

3 ...two short legs and feet,

4 ...a long arm and hand and a little one!

5 Now draw in his eyes, ears and mouth.

6 Add a row of buttons to each control panel.

8

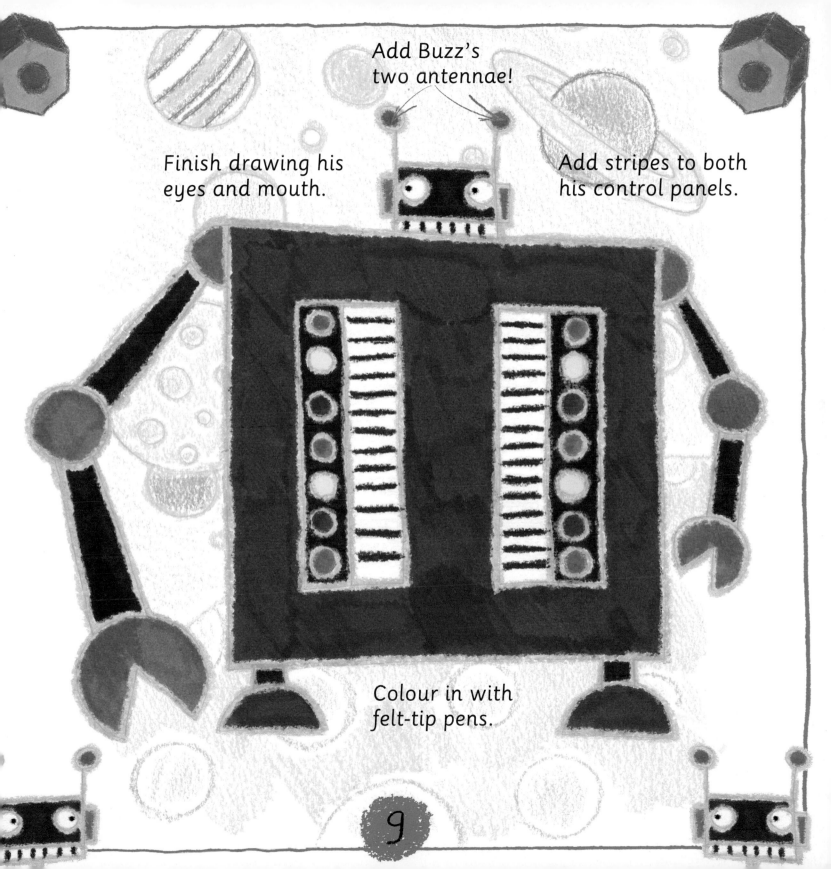

Finish drawing his eyes and mouth.

Add Buzz's two antennae!

Add stripes to both his control panels.

Colour in with felt-tip pens.

9

Ping!

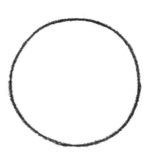

1 Ping needs a body,

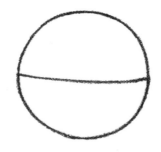

2 ...a head,

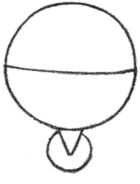

3 ...a little wheel,

4 ...and two big arms and hands.

5 Draw in Ping's face, eyes and nose,

6 ...and his mouth and two ears!

Add two wiggly, wobbly antennae.

Finish drawing Ping's eyes and mouth.

Draw in Ping's control panel and some buttons.

Colour in with felt-tip pens.

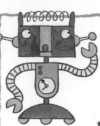

Hiss!

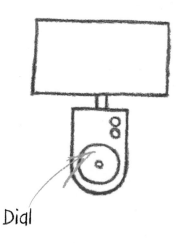

Dial

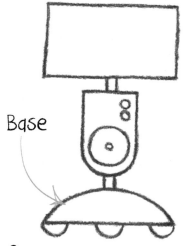

Base

1 Hiss needs a head, a neck,

2 ...and a body with a dial and two buttons.

3 Now add a base with three wheels,

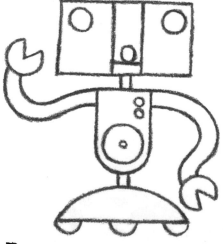

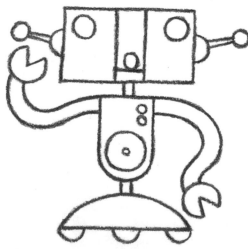

4 ...and two bendy arms and hands.

5 Draw Hiss's eyes, nose and mouth,

6 ...and add two ears and her antennae!

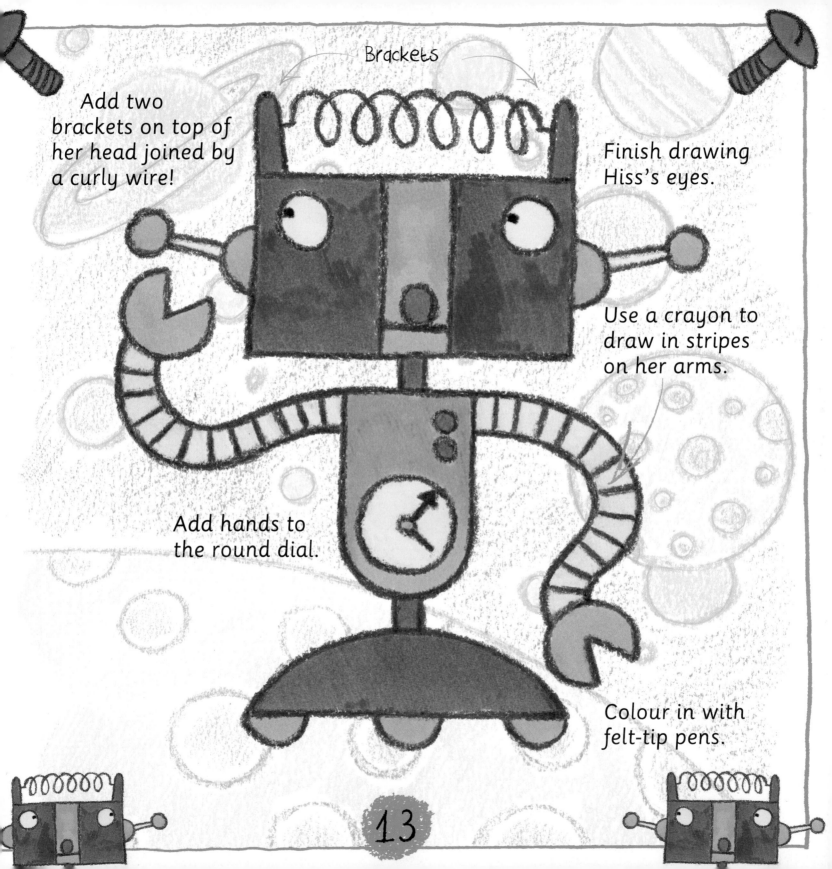

Add two brackets on top of her head joined by a curly wire!

Brackets

Finish drawing Hiss's eyes.

Use a crayon to draw in stripes on her arms.

Add hands to the round dial.

Colour in with felt-tip pens.

Whiz!

1 Whiz needs a head and neck,

2 ...a body and a control panel,

3 ...**three** legs and feet,

4 ...and two arms and hands.

5 Now draw in two eyes and a mouth,

6 ...and antennae on each side of his head!

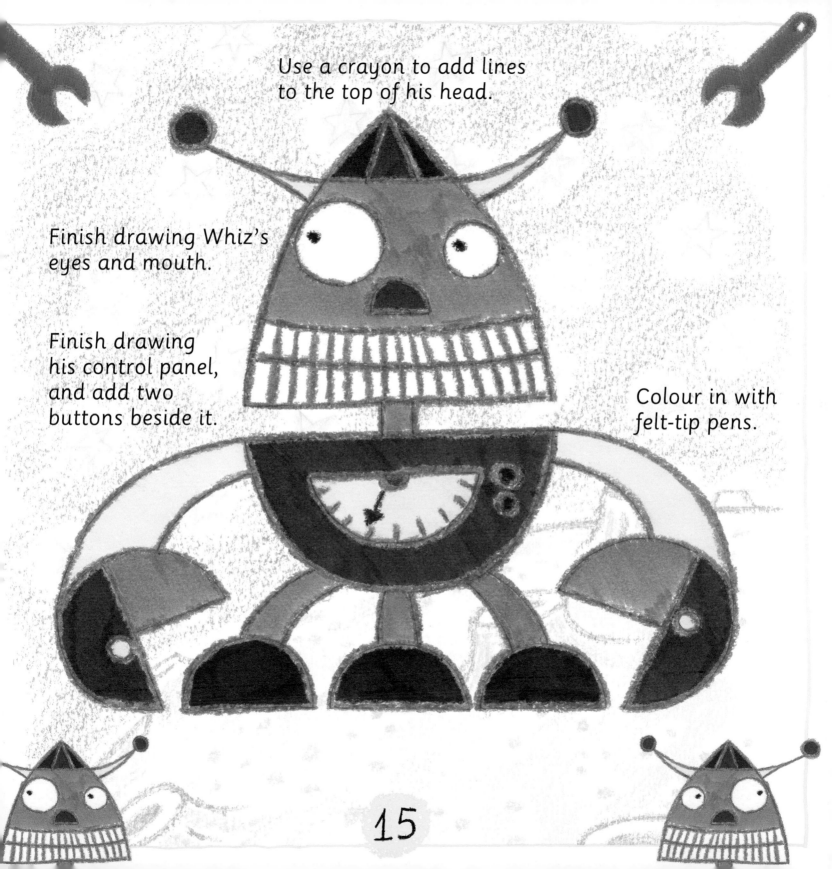

Use a crayon to add lines to the top of his head.

Finish drawing Whiz's eyes and mouth.

Finish drawing his control panel, and add two buttons beside it.

Colour in with felt-tip pens.

15

Purp!

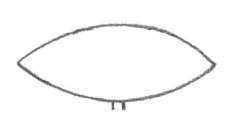

1 Purp needs a **big** head with a small neck,

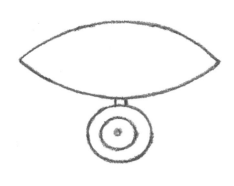

2 ...a body with a dial,

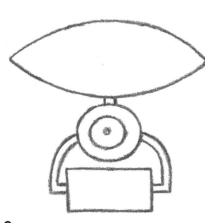

3 ...clamps and a roller,

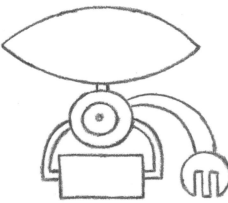

4 ...one **long** arm and a big hand,

5 ...and two small arms and hands.

6 Now draw in her eyes, nose and very wide mouth!

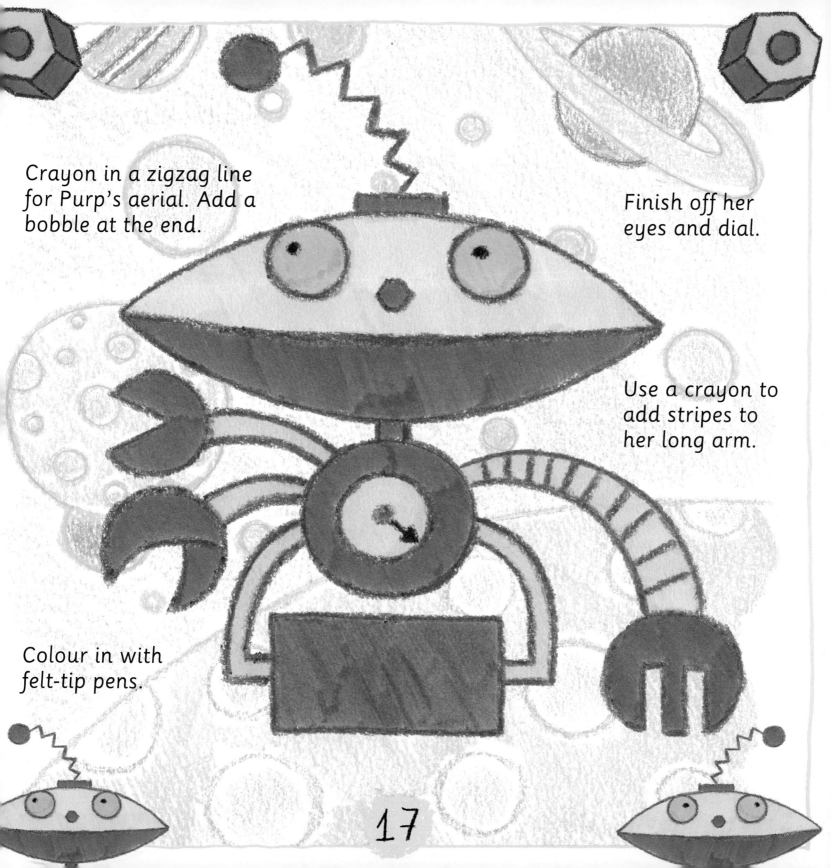

Crayon in a zigzag line for Purp's aerial. Add a bobble at the end.

Finish off her eyes and dial.

Use a crayon to add stripes to her long arm.

Colour in with felt-tip pens.

17

Bleep!

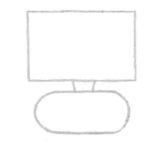

1 Bleep needs a head and neck,

2 ...a body,

Eye sockets

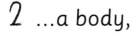

3 ...two legs and feet,

Antennae

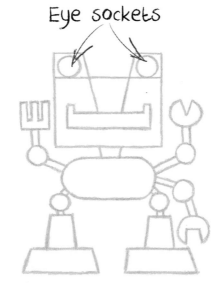

4 ...and three arms and hands.

5 Add his eye sockets, eyes, a nose and mouth,

6 ...and two ears and antennae.

Finish drawing Bleep's eyes.

Use a crayon to draw a row of buttons on Bleep's mouth.

Draw in his control panels and add stripes.

Colour in with felt-tip pens.

19

Ting!

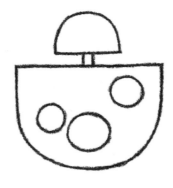

1 Ting needs a head and neck,

2 ...a **big** body with three dials,

3 ...one fat wheel,

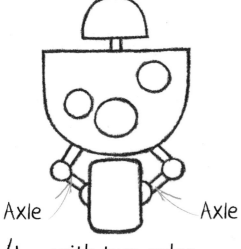

Axle   Axle

4 ...with two axles.

5 Add a big arm and hand and a small one,

6 ...and draw one big eye and her mouth.

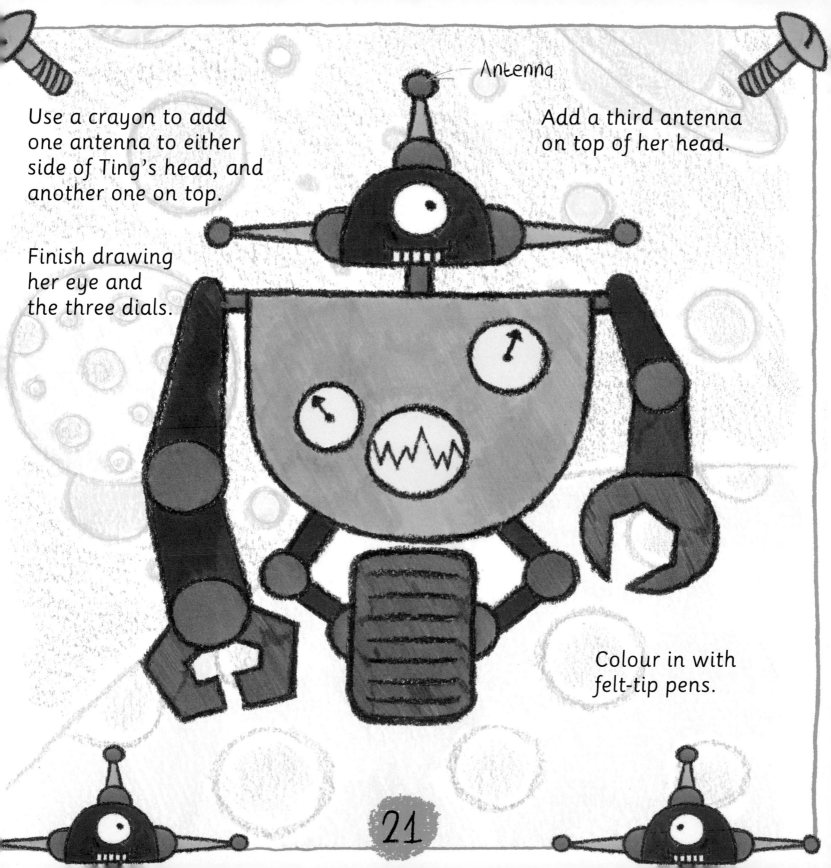

Antenna

Use a crayon to add one antenna to either side of Ting's head, and another one on top.

Add a third antenna on top of her head.

Finish drawing her eye and the three dials.

Colour in with felt-tip pens.

Zap!

control panel

1 Zap needs a head,

2 ...a body and a control panel,

3 ...legs, **knobbly** knees and feet,

Antennae

4 ...and two arms and hands.

5 Draw in her eyes, nose and mouth,

6 ...and two antennae.

Finish drawing
Zap's eyes.

Use a crayon to add
dials and switches to
her control panel.

Colour in with
felt-tip pens.

23

Clack!

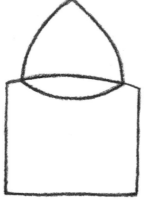

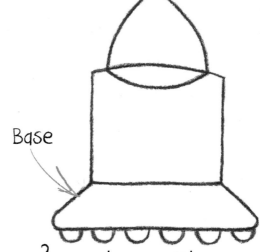

Base

1 Clack needs a head,

2 ...a square body,

3 ...a base with **six** wheels,

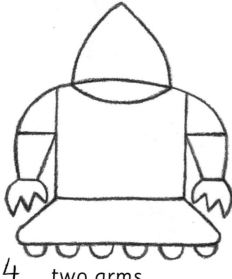

control panel

4 ...two arms and hands,

5 ...and two eyes and ears!

6 Draw in his control panel and buttons.

24

Finish drawing Clack's eyes and teeth.

Add stripes to his control panel using a crayon.

Colour in with felt-tip pens.

Tick!

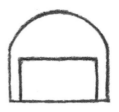

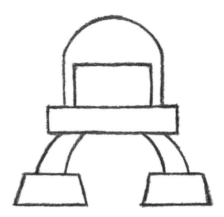

1 Tick needs a head, a box-shaped face,

2 ...a little body,

3 ...two legs with big feet,

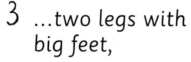

Helmet   Antennae

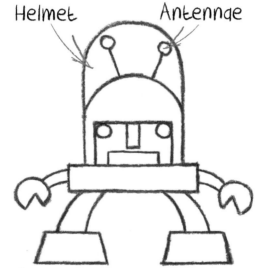

4 ...and two small arms and hands.

5 Draw in his eyes, nose and mouth,

6 ...a helmet and two antennae!

Finish drawing
Tick's eyes
and mouth.

Colour in with
felt-tip pens.

27

Tock!

1 Tock needs a head,

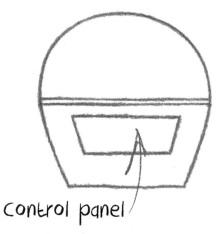

control panel

2 ...a body and a control panel,

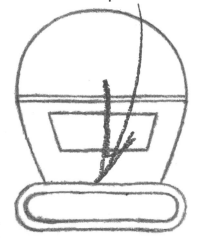

Caterpillar track

3 ...and a **caterpillar** track

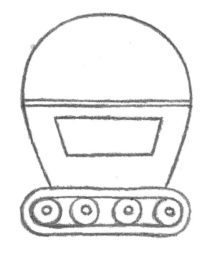

4 ...with four wheels.

5 Now draw in his two arms and hands,

6 ...two eyes, a nose and a mouth.

Aerials

Finish drawing
his eyes.

Use crayon to add
Tock's two aerials
with a zigzag line
between them.

Add stripes
to his control
panel.

Add three
buttons.

Colour in with
felt-tip pens.

Snap!

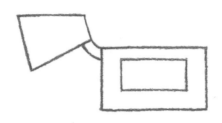

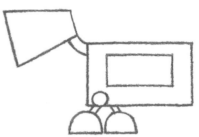

1 Snap needs a head and a neck,

2 ...a body and a control panel,

3 ...two front legs with **big** paws,

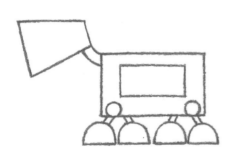

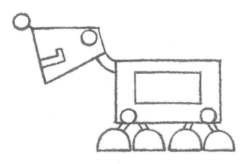

4 ...and two back legs and paws!

5 Draw in his eye, nose and mouth,

6 ...and his two ears and zigzag tail.

Draw in Snap's teeth and add his eye.

To finish his control panel, use a crayon to add stripes, a dial and some buttons.

Colour in with felt-tip pens.

glossary

Antennae *feelers.*

Axle *the rod that a robot's wheels are mounted on.*

Caterpillar track *a loop of metal or rubber plates that helps a robot to travel on rough ground.*

Control panel *the part of a robot (or other machine) that has switches or buttons to tell the robot what to do.*

Dial *a device like a clock face that gives information about speed, pressure, etc.*

Eye sockets *the parts of a robot's or animal's head that the eyes fit into.*

Helmet *a hard hat to protect the head.*

Roller *a very wide wheel for use on smooth ground.*

index